CHRIST IN SESSION

An Introduction to the Body of Christ

BOB MUMFORD

An honest attempt to remove the obscurity and vagueness surrounding the term "Body of Christ." It may give you a new grip on the purpose for your own Christian life!

BOB mumford

Box 22341 • Ft. Lauderdale, Florida 33315 • (305) 524-3349

ACKNOWLEDGEMENTS

Special thanks must be expressed to Janet Baum, whose editorial assistance in the preparation of this book exemplifies the principles of "Body Concepts" set forth in its pages.

May my indebtedness toward fellow ministers, to the Lord Himself, and to His Body on the earth, be evident to all who read *CHRIST IN SESSION*.

ISBN 0-8007-8132-5

CONTENTS

OTHER BOOKS BY BOB MUMFORD

"Living Happily Ever After"

Based on the popular audio and video tapes of the same title, this excellent book is designed to bring about a genuine cure for a troubled marriage, and provide some valuable marriage counseling guidelines.

"Take Another Look at Guidance"

A Bible study that reads like a novel! Because it is loaded with biblical references and illustrations, it should prove to be a spiritual life-saver, offering "how to's" on divine guidance.

"The Problem of Doing Your Own Thing"

The written version of the tape series entitled, "The Nature and Spirit of Obedience." If obeying is your problem, or you desire to minister to others along these lines, this book will do it!

"15 Steps Out"

Discover a way of life with meaning and fulfillment. If you are disillusioned with routine church life, and are confused by the rapid changes occurring in churches today, this book will dispell your confusion.

"A Psalm For Living"

A practical study in Psalms 22, 23 and 24, portraying the Christian walk and ministering encouragement and comfort, unfolding a deeper understanding of God's plan and purpose for believers.

These *books and other interesting subjects available on Audio-Cassette* from:

P.O. Box 22341
Ft. Lauderdale, Florida 33315

INTRODUCTION

"You can't build a tree — you have to grow one."

This simple statement was made in a discussion regarding the nature of the Church. It reverberated through the halls of my soul long after it had been expressed.

Like a tree, the Body of Christ — by its very nature — cannot be built, fabricated — or, in fact, organized. It is an organism, born in fellowship.

There has been so much literature published which pertains to the Church and its related subjects that I hesitate to write lest I add to the confusion and not to understanding. However, this book, written for the average believer in the Lord Jesus Christ, presents one image of many — *Christ in Session* — hoping to introduce you to a concept and understanding that will affect your daily life.

The need to functionally comprehend the Body of Christ is critical. Spiritual realities are being demanded of the Christian faith which she must be able to produce or she will be relegated to "just another philosophy". The cry which I hear everywhere in this computerized day is the cry to *belong!*

Substitutes for Christian reality continue to arise

in the secular realms. Psychology and psychiatry offer group therapy and sensitivity training; cults offer pseudo-love and relationship; there are even government-sponsored programs designed to meet needs in this area. These are supposed to meet moral, ethical and spiritual needs — demonstrating the failure of the Church.

The following prayer expresses the heart-cry of many within the Body today.

> *Bound by tradition,*
> *Chained of her own volition,*
> *Her ancient birthright sold,*
> *Her early fires cold,*
> *The Church, in self-made bondage lies*
> *Powerless, beneath times' threatening skies.*
>
> *Unless this yoke she breaks away,*
> *She'll not regain the Spirit's sway;*
> *In courage she has yet to face*
> *Her prejudice, her great disgrace.*
>
> *She need not stay a stunted dwarf.*
> *But, like a conquering giant come forth,*
> *If she will break tradition's chain,*
> *And free her Pentecostal flame*
> *In liberating power she*
> *Can rise to set the nations free.*
>
> *Forgive, O Lord, the centuries' sin,*
> *Come, Holy Ghost — O come within!*
>
> M.A.G., New Zealand.

There can never be an effectual substitute for the fellowship and placement offered to us within the pages of the New Testament. This is reality. How to gain that in our day is what this book is all about.

The strong bands of tradition, both good and bad — Roman Catholic and Protestant — hold the Church in a grip which only the power of God's Holy Spirit could possibly break. As I understand it, this is indeed what is happening as a result of the present day outpouring of the Holy Spirit.

My question to you, dear reader, is this: How can every other science, form of communication, discipline, institution and structure go through almost total change in the past fifty years — and the Church of Jesus Christ go on conducting "Business As Usual"?

She *must* change — and that change, I believe, will come from more clearly understanding the Body of Christ and its function on this earth.

O God, Father of our Lord Jesus Christ,
Grant us — this reader and me — the joy
of Communicating in Spirit and truth.
In Jesus Name — Amen.

Bob Mumford

Chapter One

PROBLEM . . . SHADOW OR SUBSTANCE?

I want reality — don't you? I want it in every area and operation of my life. I want it in my family life . . . in my business relations . . . at social gatherings . . . and in the spiritual realm. How do I go about accomplishing this objective? How can I tell what is "for real" and what is merely a shadow of the real? Is it possible that in any or all of these relationships in life I have only been experiencing a shadow of the real? Could this be why my heart continues to cry out for something I can embrace that will give me satisfaction for the daily demands of life?

Like many in our day, I travel quite a bit. When I come home from a long trip what a welcome sight it is to have my wife meet me at the door. I see her standing there — beside her is a shadow. Which do you think I go for? Do I run up and grab the shadow and say, "Oh Honey, it's good to see you!" If I do, I soon find there is nothing there — my arms are just wrapped around a blob of nothing. Can it be that in our seeking for reality we have reached for the shadow and left the "real" standing alongside waiting to be recognized?

I met the Lord in a church in Atlantic City, New Jersey. The church had stairs leading directly from the entrance down to a street level. As I came out of the church that morning, I was smiling and happy. I was a sailor at the time and didn't yet understand all that had happened to me, but I knew it was something real and definite. A·woman standing at the bottom of those church steps said to me, "Bob, you have given your heart to Jesus. The day is coming when the things of Christ will be more real to you than this street."

My immediate reaction was, "Oh, brother!" Looking down that street, I thought, "The things of Christ more real than this street? Impossible!" But upon returning to the church a year and a half later on a visit and coming down those steps again, I looked at the street — and it suddenly dawned on me that her prophetic word had become a reality in my life. The things of Jesus had become so real to me that I knew I possessed the unseen and the eternal within me, and that the street was only the seen and temporal. How did this come about? It wasn't all at once — it was a growing experience.

One of the first and most necessary steps is to discover *for oneself* what is for real and what is not. As I was reading and studying the Old Testament, I saw a temple and a tabernacle . . . an ark with candlesticks, mercy seat, the veil. It all seemed so concrete that I found myself saying, "I like reality."

But I was surprised to have the Lord say to me, "No, Bob, that is not the substance of the thing — that is the shadow. I AM REALITY."

My response was, "But, I thought the unseen was the shadow!"

That's the way it seemed at times. I would look

up into the sky and want to shout, "God, why don't you just step out of the clouds and say, 'Hey, Bob, it's me, God!' " If we will be honest with ourselves and others, we will all admit to times like this.

An Old Testament prophet who did his best to bring the people of his day into a sense of reality was Jeremiah. Hear him as he speaks this message to them from Jehovah God:

> *And I will give you leaders after my own heart, who will guide you with wisdom and understanding . . . you will no longer wish for the 'good old days of long ago' when you possessed the ark of God's covenant . . . for the Lord himself will be among you.* (Jeremiah 3:15–17, Living Bible)

Imagine someone brave enough to tell the Jewish people there would ever be anything more real than the Ark and the Tabernacle!

In the New Testament Paul also tried to bring to those of his generation the reality of Christ by contrasting Him to the man-made and seemingly concretes of their religion:

> *So don't let anyone criticize you for what you eat or drink, or for not celebrating Jewish holidays and feasts or new moon ceremonies or Sabbaths. For these were only temporary rules that ended when Christ came. They were only shadows of the real thing — of Christ Himself.* (Colossians 2:17, Living Bible)

Is it possible that one of the greatest snares in coming into the *real* is religion? Yes, I think it is. For so long we have presented substance in the form of the concretes — brick and mortar . . .

church buildings, duly constituted and denominationally oriented structures, rules and regulations . . . do this, don't do that. We run to these concrete substances, cling to them, try to build on them. Yet, reality most often eludes us. Somehow the deep cry in our spirits for reality and satisfaction cannot be met in the concrete. The concrete cannot love back; it does not respond. So we find what we thought was substance is only shadow. Where then *is* the real?

In my own search, I have found the real is the Body of Christ — the many-membered Body which God has ordained and established through which He can express Himself and make Himself real. Remember Jeremiah's word, ". . . for the Lord himself will be among you"; and Paul's, ". . . They were only shadows of the real thing — of Christ Himself." Another thing which I discovered was that there were many others across the land and around the globe who had found this same truth. *Reality is found in the Body of Christ!*

This is nothing really new — it is just new to some of us who have been trying for a long time to fight our way out of the shadows. It is what Paul found in his searching. For many years he had been grasping for reality in the "concretes" of his Jewish heritage and training. He found that which he had been embracing was not satisfying his needs. Then he met Jesus Christ on the road to Damascus and he knew, "This is for real!" He spent the rest of his life seeking to make it real to others.

This is exactly what I am trying to do. My desire is to communicate to others the substance which is present in the intimate group structure God or-

dained when He said: "Where two or three are
gathered together in my name, there am I!" Here,
with others who are part of the many-membered
fellowship of the Body of Christ, we find love and
response and true substance.

Psychology offers substitutes for the benefits of
this intimate group structure God instituted.
Group therapy and sensitivity training are pat-
terned along these same principles. In such settings
it soon becomes apparent how really sensitive one
is! But when a person comes together *with others
of the Body of Christ,* Christ Himself is present to
bring out the sensitive areas and to show us what
we can do to bring them into true alignment with
His desires for us.

As people meet in these sharings, one thing we
are apt to find is that we have to admit there is
dwelling in each of us more than one "self". Most
discover we have four selves — the business
self . . . the church self . . . the social self . . .
and the one who goes home at 5:30 P. M.! Let's be
as honest as we might be in a small gathering and
look at some of the shadows of our real "self".

How about the shadow who goes out into the
business world — whether it be executive office,
machine shop or to the super-market. Is the
bravado we sometimes display pure camouflage for
an aching heart or a confused mind? Then there is
the shadow who goes off to parties . . . the golf
course . . . the pizza parlor. We can appear the life
of the party or the proverbial wall-flower without
truly expressing the real "me". Moving closer to
home — is the one who gets up in the morning . . .
sits down to meals . . . mows the lawn or makes

the beds — is this only a reasonable (and at times unreasonable!) facsimile of the self we long to be? Still another "self" gets dressed up on Sunday morning and goes off for spiritual refueling. A certain pew . . . a special hymn . . . nodding to fellow members . . . a hand-shake from the preacher on the way out. Has reality been a part of any of these mechanics?

The world has been watching closely these masks that Christians put on and take off according to occasion and demand. It is not any more satisfying to them than it is to us. They are asking themselves — is this reality? It bears the label of religion — is this all there is to it? Am I supposed to buy that?

Yes, we can go on with "business as usual" in the spiritual realm and continue living behind the barriers we have erected around ourselves for protection and security — or we can say, "Lord Jesus, I want to be real in Your presence. I don't want the shadow. I want the substance. I want to take off these false fronts. Help me to be real at all times and present *one* consistent man as a testimony to the world!"

This is what God wants from us. He is waiting to hear that heart-cry and bring us out of the shadows into the reality He has provided. Then, as we gather together in small groups of believers and begin sharing, we find the masks coming off and reality being exposed. God wants to break through the false exteriors and surface the real. You cannot be spiritual alone. God has made us so that we need each other. This is the meaning and joy of being a member of one Body. This is how God has planned to meet our needs.

Sociologists tell us that man has four basic needs and these *must* be supplied. They are:

(1) Security

(2) Recognition

(3) Intimate response or love

(4) Adventure

These needs are scriptural and were placed within man by his Creator.

Yes, our Creator intended to meet every one of these needs to the fullest when He implanted them within us. And He intended them to best be met through His intended means — *in* Jesus Christ *through* the Body of Christ. You should know one thing — if you don't get satisfaction *His* way, you'll get it from the world — for you'll get it one way or another! Let me repeat — Jesus can and will supply all the basic needs of your inner man through the Body of Christ if you will permit Him to. Let's look at these needs and see how this works.

SECURITY: America is a slave to security. Our society is all bound up with armed guards at doors . . . steel bars on windows . . . electric alarms . . . tear gas. No, security is not here. Neither is it found in money, a certain political party or an "award-of-the-month" for best all-around father/mother/student! Security is not an outward thing. Do you recall the Psalmist saying, "Some trust in horses, others in chariots, but we shall trust in the name of our Lord"? In the midst of insecurity, there comes something that only God can supply.

Do you know where I have found security? In

the Body of Christ. I find it with my brothers who love me enough to correct and rebuke me. The knowledge that if I were sick or couldn't pay my bills, the members of the Body of Christ would come to my rescue gives me confidence and peace. Church attendance is to be desired; however, security is not found in church attendance alone, but *it depends on being rightly related to the Body of Christ.* It is being surrounded with fellow Christians who love you enough to correct you when you are in error and who are there to strengthen you in time of trouble.

RECOGNITION: This need is built in by God. It, too, can be supplied through the Body. Jesus taught on the ultimate in recognition when He told us that one day we can stand before the Father and hear Him say, "Well done, good and faithful servant." Until then, He has arranged for us to receive this recognition through others rightly related to Him and to each other. *There is a divine interchange possible as we receive from our brothers and sisters in Christ.*

This need is satisfied when we recognize each other as fellow members of the Body — for what we are and not for what we have. Have you ever met up with a brother whom you hadn't seen for some time and had him say, "Hey, it's good to see you!" Something leaps within your spirit — it is not because of anything you have, but because of the bond you share in Christ. He recognizes me and I recognize him — one in the same Body.

LOVE — INTIMATE RESPONSE: This is different

from recognition. Have you ever made the mistake of patting a stray dog on the head? It will take you three weeks to get rid of him. You don't have to feed him. He may go off somewhere else to eat but he will come back to you for love. We all need to be loved.

Sex is often equated with love. However, sex is only a small part of the basic need to be loved. God created sex as a part of the whole outworking between husband and wife. Much of the world's understanding and supply of "love" is twisted and warped. Today, the words "sexual revolution . . . love-ins . . . pads" picture this. No wonder the shadows in this area are formidable!

It isn't just in the sexual areas that shadows confuse. Shadows are evident in our churches. One can be a Christian and lack the ability to love. There can be, as well, churches without love. Paul discussed these possibilities in I Corinthians chapter 13 — the Love chapter.

The educated may feel the lack of love when he goes into a little store-front church. Or the uneducated may receive instant rebuff when he steps into the staid and formal lines drawn by the members in another church. Someone may be Black — another Mexican — still another may not be conforming in matters of dress and personal appearance. Our practices and prejudices can create an atmosphere that is not conducive to acceptance, let alone radiating an expression of love. Intimate response is a fantastic commodity and the world is starving for it.

Personally, my need for love is being supplied through right relationship to my wife and family . . . my brothers in Christ . . . the group with which we fellowship, our church family, as well as others outside this immediate circle. The moment we meet, the love of God for each other begins to flow among us . . . it is *felt* and my needs are met!

ADVENTURE: Some may think this is not a basic need in our lives because we do not actively pursue the adventuresome. It may be that we have suppressed this need and pushed it so far down within ourselves that it doesn't seem a part of our personalities. But, if we will investigate the matter, we may find that we do have these needs and are getting them met vicariously through television programs . . . the magazines or books we choose to read . . . the society or sports pages of the newspaper. Did you realize that hundreds of millions of crime magazines are sold annually because someone is vicariously getting his need for adventure filled through their pages?

When I came to the Lord, I came with an admitted need for adventure. And He has abundantly supplied in this area. The Spirit- filled life has been one adventure followed by another.

One year my family and I traveled through Las Vegas on our way to California. We walked down that world-famous gaudy main street with its lights flashing — jangling noises and loud laughter ringing in the air. We looked into hotels and watched the people caught in a frenzy as they put money into the slot machines — descriptively called "One Armed Bandits". My wife and I looked at each other and she said to me, with tears rimming her eyes, "Honey, aren't you glad we are not a part of this?" We were overwhelmed with gratitude to God that He had given us a more perfect way of supplying our need for *adventure*.

Yes, I am glad that in a day when most of the world is gripped in insecurity there is a people who are finding security in the Body of Christ. I rejoice that in the struggle for recognition, there are those who find this need met through looking to their Father and to the Body of Christ. I am grateful, too, that He has arranged for the intimate response and flow of love I need, as well as providing in the area of adventure. He has offered us *substance*. There is no need to be satisfied with *shadow*.

Alright, now that we have become conscious of some areas in our lives where shadow and substance may have been vieing for control, permit me to outline some suggestions for evaluating the situation and moving into reality.

FIVE WAYS TO REJECT THE SHADOW AND EMBRACE THE REAL

1. Recognize your need.

Emptiness or loneliness in the midst of a crowd is a symptom not to be overlooked.

False identities and the need to create impressions signal the fact that you have not embraced the real.

Complacency is deadly.

Mary, the mother of Jesus said, ". . . he hath filled the hungry with good things; and the rich hath sent *empty* away" (Luke 1:53).

2. Re-examine the foundation of your Christian walk.

In order to move forward in the Christian experience, especially in relationship, there needs to be a proper and secure foundation beneath the person who is searching for spiritual reality. This foundation consists of three aspects of one experience.

(a) You should have a clear understanding of Jesus Christ as the Lamb of God, Who is your Saviour. Forgiveness of sin and a life free from condemnation is a pre-requisite to participation in the Body relationship (John 1:29).

(b) You should have in your possession a valid, satisfying experience of water baptism by immersion (Acts 2:38).

(c) You should have embraced Jesus Christ as the One Who baptizes in the Holy Spirit. A free-flowing experience in prayer and worship, both in understanding and in a heavenly language is important (I Corinthians 14:15).

3. Hold to the Headship of Christ.

There is a clear organic relationship in the Body of Christ which is supplied by a new recognition of the Headship of Christ.

In a simple act of faith and obedience, confess Jesus as the Lord and functional Head for you, personally, and for your home and family. Receive Him, as well, as the Head of your group, fellowship and church. Finally, confess Him as Lord and Head of the whole Body of Christ here and in the nations of the world.

Understanding this and confessing it connects us in a life-giving way to the Lord Jesus and each other (Colossians 1:24, 2:19).

4. Place your emphasis on relationship.

For years, the church as a whole, has been impressed with large churches and big crowds. The Lord, as I understand it, begins from the other end. How can we have a functional Body when we gather in the larger group, if it has not been worked out on the most basic levels?

Consider the husband/wife relationship as the very basic cellular structure of the Body of Christ — nucleus and its surrounding protoplasm. If these two are not in agreement (Ephesians 5:31–32) when the Body of Christ does come together, it is infected with a form of "Cellulitis".

Jesus taught us in Matthew 18 that we should begin with two or three. Get these into some form of harmony and, Jesus said, "I will be present, and I will answer their requests."

I suggest, to move from shadow to reality, that after you establish a right relationship to your own mate/family, find or begin a cell group — not to make a new church or hold another meeting, but for the purpose of fellowship. Don't be religious, or too introspective — just fellowship — with the emphasis on learning how to come into relationship with the Lord and with each other.

Read carefully the third chapter of Colossians and see the apostle's emphasis on relationship — wives . . . husbands . . . children . . . fathers . . . servants . . . masters!

5. Participate — don't dominate.

Whenever relationship is involved, we have to

deal with the two human tendencies which are always present:

(a) Those who sit, like the proverbial wall-flower — who could never come into relationship by virtue of being closed and fearful, with their talent wrapped in a napkin and neatly concealed.

(b) The dominating, gregarious and over-compensating personality — who, if not pruned and disciplined, will destroy all hope of relationship.

Opening those who are closed, along with the pruning of those who dominate, is part of the adventure!

What's next for me as I make the move from shadows to substance? Do words like relationship . . . the Body of Christ . . . cell group . . . fellowship, represent anything alive and vital — or are they just more empty syllables strung together? How do I go about establishing reality within this context?

The answer to these legitimate questions is found in John 14:6, where Jesus told seeking people in His generation, "I am the way, the truth and the life." We are going to take a look at the *way* He brought about reality through His life, death and resurrection. We are going to see the *truth* He taught take form and move about throughout all time and over all the earth. We desire to experience His *life* as we lay hold on the concept of *CHRIST IN SESSION*.

Chapter Two

PREPARATION . . . FOR JESUS' DEPARTURE

In order to see the reality of CHRIST IN SESSION, we must first see reality in Jesus — the man Who walked the shores of the Sea of Galilee . . . Who came heralding the Kingdom of God . . . Who performed miracles of healing and deliverance . . . Who walked upon the water and fed thousands of eager listeners from five loaves and two fish. We must sit where He sat and listen to Him discussing with His disciples some of the plans of His Father for them — and through them, for you and me.

In reading the gospels we learn that multitudes followed Jesus during the three years of His earthly ministry. Many of them saw reality in Him and sought Him out to learn more of the source of the *power* that was evident in His miracles, the source of the *authority* with which He taught, and the source of strength from which He drew His *character*. Nicodemus, a member of the Jewish Sanhedrin, came to Him by night. Zacchaeus, a tax collector, climbed a tree to get a look at Him. Mary, Martha and Lazarus entertained Him in their home and the sisters claimed the reality of His power in the time of their need — the death of their brother.

We also read of an incident where some men, who were not of the Covenant people — men who were considered heathen by the Jews — came seeking to see this teacher who spoke with evident authority. This is related in John, chapter 12:

> *And there were certain Greeks among them that came up to worship at the feast: The same came therefore to Philip (one of the disciples), which was of Bethsaida of Galilee, and desired him, saying, Sir, we would see Jesus. Philip cometh and telleth Andrew: and again Andrew and Philip tell Jesus.*

Before we read Jesus' reply to His disciples, let me ask you two questions. What if some men came to you or me asking to see Jesus. We cannot take them into the presence of the Teacher, or can we? Do we have any recourse or resources today to meet the inquiries of men who come seeking reality in Jesus? My answer to both of these questions is an unqualified *Yes.* It is the purpose of this book to unfold just how the man Jesus provided for us, His followers, to meet the inquiries of today's seeking people. A key to that provision lies in the reply Jesus made to Andrew and Philip.

> *And Jesus answered them, saying, The hour is come that the Son of man should be glorified.*

This announcement, "the hour is come . . ." is the first time that Jesus publicly proclaimed that a turning point had arrived in His life. As soon as the question brought by the Greeks was verbalized, Jesus knew that He must begin to prepare His disciples for His departure from the earth. Jesus was well aware of the fact that it was going to be extremely difficult for them to *see* what was involved in His going away.

SINGLE VISION IS VITAL

Right here we need to consider another statement which Jesus made — this one to Nicodemus when he had come seeking truth:

> *Except a man be born again, he cannot see the Kingdom of God.*

It should be an accepted fact that the natural man is blinded to spiritual truth. He cannot see what God is doing. However, just because a man *is* born again and moves from the natural realm into the spiritual — this does not insure instant 20/20 vision. Instead, it merely marks the "opening of the spiritual eyes". Vision must be developed. One must learn to focus, adjust and interpret images registered upon his "seeing apparatus". Vision, too, can become blurred and distorted by sin, tradition, religion and "foreign objects", if these are not removed.

For example, if we were to make a survey by going into some churches, groups — or even approach believers on an individual basis, how many different answers would we get to the question, "What do you *see* God doing today?"

Many people do not know that God is doing anything — or, at least, anything different than He ever did. To some He is just a benevolent provider. To others He is encased within the pages of the Bible. Those who do try to bring Him into the affairs of today might answer: "What do you mean? Don't you know the anti-Christ is coming? . . . The communists are gaining a foothold . . . Things are bad and they are going to get worse." Yes, most people are not aware of what God is up to — or even that He is up to anything unusual!

To help us understand something of the individual's responsibility in developing the ability to see God and what He is doing, we can take a lesson from two Old Testament prophets.

When Elijah was preparing for his departure from the earth, he asked Elisha, "What do you want from me?" The reply was, "I want a double portion of what you have." Elijah then made a rather unusual remark: "If you *see* me when I am taken, then your request will be granted."

The continuing story (II Kings 2:1—15) tells us that in the midst of the excitement of the coming of the fiery chariot, Elisha kept his eyes on only one thing — the figure of Elijah. Due to this faithfulness, the mantle of Elijah fell upon his seeking servant. The result of this "seeing" was performance of twice as many miracles as Elijah had performed.

Do you catch something in this incident that we need to understand? *Single vision* is necessary to seeing spiritual truths. We must keep our eyes on Jesus Christ in order to see what God is doing today.

We find that Jesus, too, was a man of single vision. His eyes were always upon His Father. These words are a portion of His reply in John chapter 12:

> *Jesus cried and said, He that believeth on*

*me, believeth not on me, but on him that sent
me. And he that seeth me seeth him that sent
me . . . For I have not spoken of myself, but
the Father which sent me, he gave me a commandment, what I should say, and what I
should speak.*

PERIPHERAL VISION IS VITAL

What did Jesus see ahead? To what was He referring when He said the Father had given Him
commandment? We need to realize that God had,
from the very beginning of His creative works, a
desire to make Himself known to man — to have a
people after His own heart. As we watch Him move
from Genesis through Revelation, we stand in awe
of His love, patience and plans. First we move into
the Old Testament to catch a vision of His work-
ings.

In Isaiah 53:6, we find a familiar verse:

*All we like sheep have gone astray, we have
turned every one to his own way; and the
Lord hath laid on him the iniquity of us all.*

Usually we think that it was Satan who scattered
people and caused them to go their own way. But
one day I began to recognize it was God Who was
at work. In searching further, I turned to Genesis
chapter 11. Here it tells that men were all in unity
at the Tower of Babel. God came and smote them
in the mouth, causing division, so they could not
come together again until He so decreed. Living
Bible vv. 1—9 record the momentous event this
way:

At that time all mankind spoke a single lan-

*guage. . . the people began to talk about
building a great city. . . This will weld us
together, they said, and keep us from scat-
tering all over the world. . . But when God
came down to see the city and the tower mankind was making, he said, Look! If they are
able to accomplish all this when they have just
begun to exploit their linguistic and political
unity, just think what they will do later!
Nothing will be unattainable for them. Come,
let us go down and give them different languages, so that they won't understand each
other's words. . . So, in that way, God scattered them all over the earth.*

God once again intervened in history as He
visited a group of one hundred and twenty persons
— this time in Jerusalem. These were gathered together — not for selfish purposes — but to wait for
God's coming into their midst. They were obedient
to the command of their Risen Lord. They were
meeting "in one accord", with pure motivation.
Acts 2:1–6, Living Bible, tells how God "smote
man in the mouth" for a second time. This time,
however, language became a unifying factor instead
of a divisive one. The language was of God's
initiation and the act opened the doors for the
advent of His spiritual kingdom in the earth. It was
part of the plan Jesus was unveiling when He told
His disciples that He spoke only as the Father gave
Him commandment. Here is part of that commandment:

*Seven weeks had gone by since Jesus' death
and resurrection, and the Day of Pentecost
had now arrived. As the believers met to-*

gether that day . . . everyone was filled with the Holy Spirit and began speaking in languages they didn't know, for the Holy Spirit gave them this ability . . . Many godly Jews were in Jerusalem . . . and were stunned to hear their own languages being spoken by the disciples.

We must *see* in these two events something of the overall design God had in mind regarding His relationship to man. His ceaseless working throughout history has been to establish here on earth an image of Himself. "In the fullness of time", Jesus came to live among us for thirty-three years. During that time He prepared a group of people who would continue living His life when He returned to the Father. This is CHRIST IN SESSION – *GOD AMONG MEN.*

Do you know what would happen if *sinners* could get together in unity? God knew what the outcome of such a coalition would be when He intervened in their plans at the Tower of Babel. This is exactly why the Communists are fighting among themselves. God breaks today's unity just as He did in Babylon when men conspired to promote their own evil desires. God permits no people – no groups – to come together except when they are purely motivated. This is true in every realm of operation throughout every age. Scientists, philosophers, doctors, theologians, denominations – few, if any, can agree within their own ranks.

God has divided men by mountains, oceans and languages. He has divided them economically, racially, and in every possible way, to keep them from coming together to promote selfish purposes.

All these things will continually cause conflict among men until the day that we come together in Jesus. Then suddenly, color means nothing . . . social status means nothing . . . denomination means nothing. We come together in Christ. However, the only way we can have unity is if we come together with a pure motivation. Otherwise there are, and always will be, splits and divisions everywhere — except where men come in true spiritual unity.

Many new fellowship groups come together with this perfect unity. Everything goes well until the motivation changes, deviating to the right or left. Then God breathes on that fellowship and scatters them. One person says, "I'm going this way." Another says, "I'm going that way." Soon the whole group splits up. *When God divides, He divides for our safety and His protection.*

So complete is this matter of division that Jesus said, in effect, "If you can get two or three gathered together in my name, I will come in the midst of them" (Matthew 18:20). "In my name", metaphorically means, "In one soul". When Christians are "one soul" in believing God, it is so pleasing to Him that He says, "I, Myself, will be there."

God structured the New Testament Church so that we would need each other. He has designed it in such a way that it cannot function except when we are in spiritual unity. John 16:7 is the crux of our understanding the New Testament Church:

> *Nevertheless, I tell you the truth: It is important for you that I go away; for if I go not away, the Comforter will not come unto you; but if I depart, I will send Him unto you.*

Notice, Jesus' emphasis on *you.* His interest is in people. Also, notice that when the Holy Spirit comes, He doesn't come in some nebulous way — He comes to *people.* Jesus said, "I will send Him unto *you."* And when the Holy Spirit came that first time on the Day of Pentecost, He did not come to the entire City of Jerusalem, He came to the one hundred and twenty expectant people there in the Upper Room, who were "in one accord" — unity!

How did this unity come about? It is important to note that the eleven disciples who were with Jesus when He said, "My hour is come . . ." formed the nucleus of that group to whom the Whole Christ first presented Himself through the coming of the Holy Spirit. Jesus' words, "I will send the Comforter . . . He shall glorify me, for He shall take of mine and show it unto you . . ." were fulfilled — and unity resulted.

JESUS' PREPARATION
FOR "CHRIST IN SESSION"

We rejoin Jesus and His disciples and listen in as He talks with them for the last time before His arrest and crucifixion. Read John chapters 13 through 17 for the entire conversation. For our study, we shall consider some questions and answers from their discussion. Beginning with John 13:33, the dialogue went something like this:

JESUS: Little children yet a little while I am with you. Ye shall seek me; and as I said unto the Jews, Whither I go, ye cannot come; so now I say to you. A new commandment I give unto you, That ye love one another; as I have loved you, that ye also love one another. By this shall all men know that ye are my disciples, if ye have love one to another.

Love is the hallmark of the Kingdom of God. Love was the motivating force in the life of Jesus. He knew these men He was leaving would soon desperately need this same kind of love and concern for one another. He knew, too, that this kind of love could only be supplied through the supernatural channels He was about to initiate.

SIMON PETER: Lord, whither goest thou?

JESUS: Whither I go, thou canst not follow me now; but thou shalt follow me afterwards.

PETER: Lord, why cannot I follow thee now? I will lay down my life for thy sake.

JESUS: Wilt thou lay down thy life for my sake? Verily, verily I say unto thee, the cock shall now crow, till thou hast denied me thrice. Let not your heart be troubled: ye believe in God, believe also in me. In my Father's house are many mansions: if it were not so, I would have told you. I go to prepare a place for you, And if I go and prepare a place for you, I will come again, and receive you unto myself; that where I am, there ye may be also. And whither I go ye know, and the way ye know.

The Greek word which Jesus used when He said, "In my Father's house . . ." is the word meaning "household" or "family". It is the same word used by Paul in Acts 16:31 when he said to the Philippian jailer, "Thou shalt be saved, and thy house." *Also, the Greek word translated in the King James Version as* mansions *means abiding place — or better still,* placement. *Jesus might have said it this way, "In my Father's family (or Body, for the Body of Christ is the Father's family on earth) are many placements — there is a place for everyone regardless of age, sex, color, background. There is a place in the Body of Christ for every one of His children!" Can you see that Jesus was attempting to get these men to see that as He goes away to prepare a placement for them, He has in mind their continuing His work?*

THOMAS: Lord, we know not whither thou goest, and how can we know the way?

JESUS: I am the way, the truth and the life; no man cometh unto the Father but by me. If ye had known me, ye should have known my Father also; and from henceforth ye know him and have seen him.

> *Even after three years of close association with Jesus, these men still had not grasped the truth that He was the express image of the Father.*

PHILIP: Lord, show us the Father, and it sufficeth us.

JESUS: Have I been so long time with you, and yet hast thou not known me, Philip? He that hath seen me hath seen the Father, and how sayest thou then, Show us the Father? Believe me that I am in the Father and the Father in me: or else believe me for the very work's sake. Verily, verily, I say unto you, He that believeth on me, the works that I do

shall he do also; and greater works than these shall
he do: because I go unto my Father.

After Jesus went to His Father, and was
revealed as CHRIST IN SESSION, were these
words fulfilled? Because of His many mem-
bered Body, Jesus is now able to operate —
not confined to one place — but He can be in
a myriad of places at the same time! Greater
works? Not just a few miracles in one day —
but many!

JESUS: If ye love me, keep my commandments,
and I will pray the Father, and He shall give you
another Comforter, that he may abide with you for
ever.

Here Jesus introduces the Holy Spirit who
would be the ever present source of Jesus'
power, authority *and* strength *available to*
them forever. In the Greek, there are two
words for our one English word "another".
(1) allos means another of the same kind;
(2) heteros means another of different kind.
Jesus said, "I will give you another (allos)
Comforter, who is the same kind as I am, and
He will always be with you."

JESUS: Yet a little while, and the world seeth
me no more. But ye see me: because I live, ye shall
live also . . . and I will manifest myself to him.

Here again is this matter of "seeing". The
Comforter is to be a Person — He can be
known just as Jesus was known. The disciples
would see Jesus — the world would not.

JUDAS (not Iscariot): Lord, how is it that thou
wilt manifest thyself unto us, and not unto the
world?

Can you sympathize with these men? If Jesus is here, everyone can see Him. If He is not here, how can anyone see Him? These men are not wearing haloes. They are just as baffled as you and I would have been. ". . . here . . . going away . . . you will see me . . . but the world will not." Jesus took this bewilderment into consideration as He patiently unfolded His plan.

JESUS: The Comforter, which is the Holy Ghost, whom the Father will send in my name, he shall teach you all things and bring all things to your remembrance, whatsoever I have said unto you.

Aren't you glad that the disciples didn't have to learn it all in one sitting? It must have been some comfort to them to know that this Comforter would help them with the answers when Jesus was gone.

JESUS: Nevertheless I tell you the truth: It is expedient for you that I go away; for if I go not away the Comforter will not come unto you; but if I depart I will send him unto you . . . When He, the Spirit of truth, is come, he will guide you into all truth . . . he shall glorify me: for he shall receive of mine, and shew it unto you. A little while and ye shall not see me: and again, a little while, and ye shall see me, because I go to the Father.

How many of us really understand this even now? Imagine hearing it for the first time!

THEN SAID THE DISCIPLES AMONG THEM-SELVES: What is this that he saith unto us, A little while . . . what is this . . . we cannot tell what he saith.

Notice they said this among themselves —

not to Jesus! Have you ever had this same
thing happen? In school the teacher puts a
math problem on the board and says, "Every-
body understand this?" And the pupils
answer, "Yes, Teacher." Then out in the hall-
way they all begin to ask each other, "What
did he mean . . . I don't get it!"

NOW JESUS KNEW THAT THEY WERE DE-
SIROUS TO ASK HIM AND SAID: Do you en-
quire among yourselves of that I said, A little
while, and ye shall not see me: and again, a little
while and ye shall see me?

But Jesus did not leave them questioning.
He brought the dialogue to a close with these
words.

JESUS: I came forth from the Father, and come
into the world: again, I leave the world and go to
the Father.

DISCIPLES: Lo, now speakest thou plainly . . .
Now are we sure that thou knowest all things, and
needest not that any man should ask thee: by this
we believe that thou camest from God.

Knowing that Jesus came from God, the
disciples were content to trust the Father and
their confidence was rewarded when they saw
the resurrected Jesus, the coming of the Com-
forter, and through these two events, they
were to become part of the Body of Christ on
earth — which is CHRIST IN SESSION.

JESUS SHOWS ME CHRIST IN SESSION

I first began seeing what Jesus was saying to His
disciples as recorded above when He revealed Him-

self to me during a service in a church in New York. As I was preaching, I looked down the aisle and saw in mental vision Jesus standing there with His arms outstretched — looking at me!

3 GIFTS OF SPEAKING
1. Tongues
2. Interpretation of Tongues
3. Prophecy

3 GIFTS OF KNOWING
1. Wisdom
2. Knowledge
3. Discerning of Spirits

← **AUTHORITY**

3 GIFTS OF DOING
1. Healing
2. Miracles
3. Faith

He revealed Himself very plainly. I saw as it were the *gifts of knowing* . . . the *gifts of doing* . . . and the *gifts of authority* resident in Him. *Healing, miracles and faith* were in His hands. *The word of wisdom and the word of knowledge and discerning of spirits* were in His head. And the *authority* of God was on His chest. This was how the concept of CHRIST IN SESSION was partly born — when I saw the Whole Christ! As He stood there, fully unveiled to me, I knew I could never be satisfied with, or settle for, anything less than this fully revealed Whole Christ. Jesus gave us Himself — His all!

Suddenly I was able to see something of what Jesus was saying to His disciples there in the Upper Room. "Do you see me, disciples, standing here with the *power* and *authority* and the *love, joy, peace?*" The disciples replied, "Yes, we see you."

Then Jesus told them, "In a little while you won't see Me *like this* anymore. I have to go to My Father. But if I go to My Father, I am going to arrange for the Holy Spirit to take everything that I am and have, and He will bring it back to you in a spiritual form. In a little while you won't see Me . . . in a little while you will see Me. How? Where two or three are gathered in My name — there I am!"

This, now, is a divine principle. How does it work? Jesus laid down this principle in John 12:24:

> *Verily, verily, I say unto you, Except a corn of wheat fall into the ground and die, it abideth alone; but if it die, it bringeth forth much fruit.*

We know a corn of wheat must be buried in the ground in order for it to multiply. All farmers plant on the principle that from one grain properly planted, a stalk comes up. On that stalk there may be three or four ears of corn; and on each ear there may be several hundred more little grains of corn. That one grain can bring into being thousands of grains of corn. Do you see this principle in operation in the death, burial, resurrection and coming of the Holy Spirit — all as outlined by Jesus?

Jesus presented another principle when He said:

> *He (the Holy Spirit) shall glorify* me: *for he*
> *shall receive of* mine, *and shall show it unto*
> *you. All things that the Father hath are* mine;
> *therefore, said I, that he shall take of* mine,
> *and shall show it unto you.*

Four times Jesus refers to Himself and His possessions — me . . . mine . . . mine . . . mine. I felt certain there must be a key to what Jesus was trying to convey here. He opened to me an understanding that proved vital in my own experience. We must see that the Holy Spirit Who came was not *another* — but was in reality Jesus Who had come in spiritual form! I want to share with you what, to me, Jesus meant when He said, "I will come to you . . . Ye shall see me . . ."

Forty days after Jesus ascended into Heaven, the Descension came as related in Acts chapter 2. At this time the Holy Spirit was outpoured. When Jesus ascended into Heaven, the Holy Spirit took all that was in Christ and brought the same to us. As He descended, He brought to us the Whole Christ.

First, we have the *character of Christ*. This is described in Galatians 5:22–23:

> *The fruit of the Spirit is love, joy peace,*
> *longsuffering, gentleness, faith, meekness,*
> *goodness, temperance.*

When a person met Jesus in the flesh, he met these nine fruit of the Spirit. *His character was love . . . joy . . . peace — all of these.* I can now say, "Oh, I understand. That is what Jesus was like." This was His *character*.

Then one day while studying the *gifts of the*

Spirit as given in I Corinthians 12:8–10:

> *For unto one is given by the Spirit the word of wisdom; to another the word of knowledge, by the same Spirit; To another faith by the same Spirit; to another the gifts of healing by the same Spirit; to another the working of miracles; to another prophecy; to another discerning of spirits; to another divers kinds of tongues; to another the inter- pretation of tongues . . .*

I began to relate this to my understanding of the character of Jesus and came to see a second truth. "Yes, I understand! As the Lord moves through the earth, *the gifts of the Spirit, the power of Christ* — that *power that was on Him* as He healed the sick and cast out devils and spoke to the waves on the Sea of Galilee — all of these things that were in Him — the spiritual manifestations evident in His ministry — these are ours! — the Holy Spirit dividing to every man as He wills!"

However, we must understand a third truth. This was brought into focus while reading Ephesians 4:11–13. Here is listed the *ministry gifts;* apostles, prophets, evangelists, pastors and teachers. Hebrews 3:1 presents Jesus as the Apostle of our faith. Jesus is also called the Prophet . . . He is the Pastor, or Shepherd. He is the greatest Teacher there ever has been. He is the Evangelist of all time. He is all of these! I saw the *authority of Christ* — this that was part of Him while He performed His earthly ministry is ours, too. And so Christ has set in the Church the *authority* that belongs to Him.

Preparation for departure was the unveiling to the disciples Jesus' plan to bestow upon them,

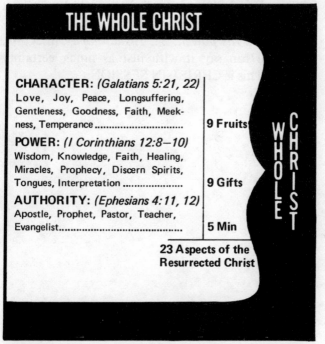

THE WHOLE CHRIST

CHARACTER: *(Galatians 5:21, 22)*
Love, Joy, Peace, Longsuffering,
Gentleness, Goodness, Faith, Meek-
ness, Temperance .... **9 Fruits**

POWER: *(I Corinthians 12:8—10)*
Wisdom, Knowledge, Faith, Healing,
Miracles, Prophecy, Discern Spirits,
Tongues, Interpretation .... **9 Gifts**

AUTHORITY: *(Ephesians 4:11, 12)*
Apostle, Prophet, Pastor, Teacher,
Evangelist... **5 Min**

**23 Aspects of the
Resurrected Christ**

WHOLE CHRIST

through the coming of the Comforter, *His character, His power,* and *His authority.* They could
not grasp the magnitude of the plan in its entirety.
Can we even now?

Listen again to Jesus saying, "You see Me standing here? In a little while you will not see Me like
this anymore. Because I go to the Father, greater
works will you do." Then He ascends in the power
of the Holy Spirit. That same Holy Spirit descends
and "divides severally as He will." Now it is Christ
UNLIMITED!

Every local church, functioning in scriptural
order, could say in that First Century, "Of a truth,
Jesus is here!" When people came to them saying,

"Sir, we would see Jesus," they could bring them into His very presence — they could see *His character* . . . *His power* . . . *His authority* in action. And we can say it with just as much certainty today! This is CHRIST IN SESSION.

Chapter Three

PROGRAM . . . FOR OPERATION

Now that we have seen the Whole Christ, our next step is to try to understand *how* He functions. The Whole Christ in operation is CHRIST IN SESSION. It involves you and me. In fact, it involves every believer in Christ.

Webster defines "session" as: "the sitting together or meeting of a group, assembly, court, legislature or council. A day-to-day series of such meetings." This pictures action . . . operation.

The words action and operation also picture CHRIST IN SESSION. It is Christ acting and operating through His divinely ordained and constituted Body here on earth. The members of the Body are vested with *authority* and *power*. They have specific responsibilities. They present to the "world" the *character* of God's Kingdom, just as earthly legislative bodies are designed to present to their constituents the character of good government. All of the day-to-day and century-by-century Kingdom business is carried out through this Body by the power of the Holy Spirit, Who is the Father's gift to us through Jesus Christ, the Son.

Christ in Session is not limited to a preacher standing in a pulpit on given days and at set times. Nor is it simply missionaries carrying the good news to foreign soil. These are man-made limitations placed upon the true intent of God's governing Body. His plan is for a twenty-four-hour-a-day, year-in-year-out operation. It is not limited to one place, period of time, or special persons. It is believers in Japan . . . Hawaii . . . Russia . . . Israel — it is everywhere and all the time! It is you — a member of His Body — in your place accepting and carrying out your part of His program on the earth.

It is my conviction that God has designed this Body so that we need each other. Every member must be involved. There are to be no spectators. There is a gift and calling for every man and woman. Even the people I don't appreciate and to whom I would not give spiritual endowments if I were the one dispensing them. In fact, that is where the excitement begins! I used to get very frustrated and say, "Lord, how can you use a person like that?" To know His ways means we have to learn some things. Just as the disciples needed to be taught the implications of Jesus' departure and return, so we need to investigate truths that may have been vague and puzzling. *His Program must be understood.*

We mentioned previously that the Englist word "another" really had two meanings in the Greek — *allos,* another of the same kind — and *heteros,* another of a different kind. In I Corinthians 12:7–12 the word "another" is used eight times. The exchange of these two Greek words shows us that God divided the spiritual gifts, not only among those who were of a similar kind and understanding, but also among those who were different in make-up and outlook. The Lord did this purposely in order to force us to appreciate one another and make it vital that we come together in spiritual unity. We need every single member of the Body of Christ for complete operation. Everyone who comes to God through Jesus Christ and is baptized in the Holy Spirit has a place and function in the Body of Christ. Listen . . .

> *To one is given, by the Spirit, the word of wisdom; to another the word of knowledge by the same Spirit; to another of a different kind faith by the same Spirit; to another the gifts of healing by the same Spirit; to another the working of miracles; to another prophecy; to another discerning of spirits; to another of a different kind divers kinds of tongues; to another the interpretation of tongues; but all these worketh that one and the selfsame Spirit, dividing to every man severally as He will. For as the body is one, and hath many members, and all members of that one body, being many, are one body, so also is Christ.*

Notice the unity of the body and the diversity of the gifts. Notice, also, that the Spirit gives "as He will" — not as I, personally, would! One of the problems in the church at Corinth, where this lesson in division was being taught by Paul, was that the members were scattered and separated. God knows that it is not in man's nature to get along with each other. Therefore, *He has divided the gifts.*

I am convinced, also, that *He has divided truth.* Each denomination and segment of the Christian Church has a certain emphasis of truth, and each particular aspect of the truth needs to be examined, shared and received by the whole Body of Christ. Many of us will not yield to what God is doing because we have managed to climb a doctrinal branch of the "truth", preventing our seeing the whole tree. I was raised in the Arminian background; but when attending an Anglican Seminary I began to see some of the truth of the sovereignty of God and other Reformed doctrines. It was a most healthy and expanding experience.

Maturity comes by learning to understand what it means to "feed on the whole counsel of God." Truth has been divided. It is not necessary to subscribe to one world church, organizationally. If we all "join one big club", that would only result in the same problems arising with which men have been grappling through the centuries. It is only as we are moving under the inspiration of the Holy Spirit, acknowledging this diversity Paul spoke of, that we can examine, share and receive from each other. Only God can bring spiritual unity; He does so within the context of pure motives on our part.

We have seen that God administers the gifts of the Spirit to many kinds of people. He gives to those of the same kind (the *allos)* and to those of a different kind (the *heteros)*. Let me give you an illustration of this truth in action.

A lady whom I know, was a real problem to her pastor, basically created by personality conflict. Actually, she was a good woman who loved the Lord with all of her heart and she sought to follow God and obey Him. One Sunday the Lord awakened her about 5:30 in the morning and said, "I want you to pray for your pastor this morning." That really disturbed her and she replied, "Lord, if this is really You, please, You make the opportunity."

That morning the church service was moving along as usual, when all of a sudden it came to a halt. The pastor leaned across the pulpit and began to weep. He was purple around the lips. His medical history included diabetes and frequent angina attacks with pain around his heart. With an urgency, he said, "Church, I am a sick man. Won't somebody obey the Lord this morning and pray for me?"

Now who in that congregation do you think he least wanted to pray for him? The Lord said to that woman, "He will refuse you, but get up and go down to pray for him." So she left that pew trembling under the power of God. That the gift of healing was upon her, there was no doubt. (Since this particular time God has used her in four similar instances and every one that she has prayed for, in obedience, has been healed. This instance was the first time God had spoken to her in this specific way.)

She walked up to the pastor. As he opened his eyes and saw her standing there, he straightened up quickly and said, "That's all right, lady, just kneel down here in prayer. Elders . . . deacons . . . come up here and pray for me!"

That woman was humiliated in front of the entire congregation. She walked back to her seat and sat down. This happened fourteen years ago and today that pastor is still a sick man. He continues to have angina symptoms and the effects of sugar diabetes. I know who has his healing! The anointing to pray for his healing remains on that woman to this day.

Does this help you to see that God has designed His Church so that we need each other? Not only do we need those of the same kind, but also those different from us. We have a strong natural tendency to gravitate to people of our temperment and liking. We form little cliques. God requires that we come out from our little self-styled gatherings and expose ourselves to the "heteros". He wants us to see that they have something to add to us. His mathematics includes addition, as well as division. Fellowship does not mean total agreement. You and I are only single "pieces" that are needed to make up the Whole Christ.

As I travel across this nation, I see fantastic things happening . . . as my spiritual eyes are opening. I see a small group of believers — a lead couple and six or eight others. Right there where they gather together in the name of Jesus and begin to worship and magnify His name — suddenly there is the quickening of the Holy Spirit which comes into that small, sedate Presbyterian prayer group. They respond to the Lord and to each other and say, "I have found it! This is what I have been searching for!"

Do you know what it is that they have found? It is Jesus come for His purpose. He comes through the operation of the Holy Spirit. He, the Holy Spirit, then divides *gifts of power* as He will to the members of that group. To one is given healing . . . to another prophesy. They begin to operate and they "see" Jesus. They can show him to others! Love, joy, peace, and all the aspects of the *character* of Christ is formed in that group. And

the power of Christ is being loosed — healings . . .
miracles . . . discernment. As He forms Himself in
them, He says, "The world will not see Me, but
you will see Me. When people come to you saying,
'Friends, we would see Jesus', you — members of
My Body — will represent Me to them." As they
proceed from this simple beginning, they recognize
the need for the *authority* of Christ, praying that
God will relate them to the ministry gifts —
Prophets . . . Pastors . . . Teachers!

On another occasion, I may meet with a small
Episcopalian prayer group and say, "Tell me, what
has the Lord been saying to you?" They respond,
"Oh, Bob, we were all seeking God and praying
and some have received the baptism in the Holy
Spirit — speaking in a heavenly language. We are
beginning to understand something about leadership. Then we started praying for the sick and
there were healings . . ."

"I see . . . I see!! I see the Body of Christ."

Do you? I see it in these groups of believers
gathering together. The ascended Christ sends the
power of the Holy Spirit into their midst and then
follows the gifts . . . the ministries . . . the operations of the Holy Spirit. These groups then relate to others in the same locality, who come together for a Believer's meeting — "when the whole
Church comes together". (I Corinthians 14:23)

Look where we have come. We have come from
One Jesus, the earthly Christ, standing in a physical
body, with the Greeks asking, "Sir, we would see
Jesus." We hear Jesus as He says in reply, "My
hour is come. I see what has to happen. I must go
to the Father so the Spirit can come . . . so in-

quiring men everywhere can see Me."

How many of you honestly see that now, under the administration of the Holy Spirit, the Whole Christ can be present in every prayer group and every local church? It is important that we understand this. Every local body . . . every local church . . . every local prayer group *can* have the whole manifestation of Christ present in their midst – active and operating!

The Whole Christ is divided to His Church.

> *He shall glorify me: for he shall receive of mine and shall show it unto you . . .*

The Holy Spirit brought Jesus back to the one hundred and twenty believers at Pentecost. They had been divided and scattered following the crucifixion of their Master. But when they came together after the Ascension of Christ, with pure motivation, in "one accord", they came together as the Body of Christ.

> *A little while and ye shall not see me . . .*
(The Ascension of Jesus into heaven.)

> *A little while and ye shall see Me . . .* (The Descension of the Holy Spirit.)

> *Sir, we would see Jesus . . .* (The Whole Christ – manifested through His people!)

When the Body comes together with pure motivation, in spiritual unity, then we see Jesus. We see His *authority*. We see His *power*. We see His *character*. What an opportunity to embrace the anointing and provision He has made possible for us in the Holy Spirit to show Christ to a seeking world. Here you will find reality!

Not only will you find reality, but you will be able to transmit reality to others. Men will come to know about *His character* — they will not have to be satisfied with reading about it on the pages of a Book. They will experience *His power* — not just thrill to the activities of an age long past. They will come under divine *authority* and recognize His Divine Lordship in the Twentieth Century — a *to-day* force, stronger than all the legislative bodies in session around the world! *Sirs, we would see Jesus* will be moved into a new dimension by ordinary people — by you and me.

Chapter Four

PROGRESS . . . OF HIS PLAN

What has happened to this divinely ordained and constituted Body over the centuries? For an answer we must look at some of the churches and groups operating in our day. They reflect the general pattern which has emerged since that First Century when the remembrance of the physical Jesus was fresh and motivating . . . and when the Holy Spirit was the activating and administrative force. Visit with me some of the gatherings of the 1970's.

An invitation comes: "Bob Mumford, why don't you come over to our church. Jesus is there."

"Oh, He is," I say. "What part of Him?"

"What do you mean, what *part* of Him" comes their response.

This response to my question might be yours, too. You may be wondering why I should ask, "What part of Him?"

In my experience I have found that most churches or groups usually *emphasize* only one of the three aspects of the Whole Christ. This often results in the utter *neglect,* and sometimes even disdain, of the other two operations which are necessary to meet the needs of people who come asking to see Jesus. Error, we discover, may be present either by over emphasis or neglect!

The first, we shall call the *Holiness-Love Group.*
These say, "We believe in personal holiness. We
believe in the fruit of the Spirit. We spend our time
cultivating love . . . joy . . . peace. We are the
truly sanctified." When I ask, "Where is the rest of
it?", they are totally unaware that something more
is needed other than just love and holy living. Have
you ever experienced how frustrating it is to love
people and not be able to do anything to help them?

Then there is the *Power Group.* Here we have the
declaration, "We believe in the gifts and power of
the Holy Ghost . . . casting out demons . . .
divine healing . . . come join with us. We have the
power of God!" This group usually has an abundance of multi-directed energy. These gift-oriented
ones are so caught up with the manifestations of
the Spirit that they neglect the love and control
that must accompany the power aspect of the
Whole Christ.

The third type of gathering is made up of those
who put their emphasis on church government and
New Testament church pattern. We might call
them *Divine Order Group.* Here we usually find an
over-abundance of deacons . . . elders . . .
prophets — all of which falls short of the true character and other two operations of the full-orbed
Christ.

The greatest fault in all of these single-track
situations is that each group thinks he "has it all"
— or at least, that he has the best and most important truth. Often this causes alienation and even
outward expressions of jealousy and enmity between the groups.

What I see the Lord Jesus doing is this: I see

Him bringing forth a Body of Christ in Atlanta . . . Los Angeles . . . Dallas — so that when a man or woman comes to any one of these places he will find expressed the Whole Christ. Then, and only then, will he find reality and satisfaction for his needs. Let me show you how handicapped a one-emphasis ministry can be.

Suppose a man comes to your group saying, "Sir, I have cancer or, my mind is blown with drugs . . . or, I am an alcoholic . . . homosexual."

Or a woman may knock at your church door and say, "I need help. I am a prostitute . . . or, my home is disintegrating . . . or, loneliness is driving me to suicide. Sir, do you have an answer for my problem?"

If the placard above your place of ministry reads *only LOVE,* you can offer that seeking person an abundance of love. You can wrap him or her in it and meet the needs in *that* area. But there is more. There may be a need for deliverance from bondage and healing of physical sickness. Will you have to say, "Sorry, but we don't minister in that area. You will have to go across town to get that taken care of."

What if that same man or woman happens to come into a group which majors on the *POWER aspect?* That needy person may get the necessary deliverance and healing and that is fine. But what about the necessary understanding of love and submission and right relationship to others in the Body? How about instruction in the divine government of the Body? If guidance in these two areas is lacking, again we have failed to portray Jesus in His fulness.

Then, if that seeking one should come into the *divine ORDER* oriented church, he might see smoothly operating government and hear the Word of God preached. There might be conviction and acceptance of Jesus as Saviour. But there is still that need to be delivered and healed — to be loved and find a place of belonging. Have these other aspects been so relegated to a corner that Christ is again segmented and lacking full expression?

Are you beginning to see *two* basic principles that must be worked into our groups and churches before they can become effective in the program Christ desires to carry out through them?

First: This program calls for every member involvement.

Second: We must present the three aspects of the Whole Christ in order to have an effective ministry.

For too many years we have tried to carry out our individual responsibility sitting in a pew looking at the back of somebody's head. We need to look each other in the eye, share our experiences, and get to know the fellow members of our particular fellowship. The time is past for being a spectator in this business of presenting Churst to our world. We must be willing to assume our share of the task — willing to accept a certain placement . . . a certain anointing or gift — and to begin to function in the Body. The Body is not one member, but many.

In order to carry out our part, we must consider:

(1) The need to see that God wants to work into us love, joy, peace, patience — all

of the *attributes of His character* into our lives.

(2) The need to know that He longs for the opportunity to *give His gifts* as He knows they will best be used to get the job done. These gifts are necessary for restoring wholeness to a lost and dying generation.

(3) The need to have our eyes opened to recognize the importance of *authority and leadership* in our midst. We need apostles and prophets and teachers sent of God. We need evangelists who are anointed to pull in the nets.

As we move from spectator to participator we will be impressed with a desire to seek God for *where* He wants us and *what* He wants us to do in bringing forth the Body of Christ in our lives. As we do this, the Holy Spirit will come to administer the gifts in our lives. Ministries will begin to flow. Love, joy, peace will be evidenced. Power, anointing, prophecy and discernment of spirits are experienced. God will give us elders, deacons and administrative gifts.

No one need be afraid of Biblical government if he is going on in God. There is a tendency to be suspicious and rebellious once one has touched the power of God. There is fear someone may take away our anointing. But government is the next thing on God's agenda. He is bringing the Church under divine apostolic, prophetic government.

Return with me, if you will, to pick up our story of the man or woman who had come seeking help in the various churches and groups we have been considering. There had been no completely satisfactory answer in any of the single-emphasis operations.

The knock comes once again at the door — the same request, "Sirs, I would see Jesus." Our response now is, "Come in. You have come to the right place." *At once he feels the love that is there.* He sees the joy and faith and peace in the lives of the members. Then comes the prophetic voice, *gifts of deliverance and healing.*

But there is still more. As that seeking one rejoices in his new-found deliverance and freedom, we tell him, "There is one more thing in our group. It is called *government."* You explain submission and love for the fellow members of the Body. The time soon comes when that one who has had all of his needs met can say, "I see Jesus in this place. I see Him in *His character . . .* in *His power . . .* in *His authority.* This is what I have been looking for — this is reality!'"

To help us move into the fullness which God desires us to know, look with me at the diagram below.

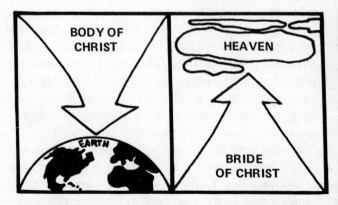

Here is pictured the two much-used names for the Church of Jesus Christ. They are: (1) the Body of

Christ; (2) the Bride of Christ. There is a definite distinction between these two.

I would like to suggest that when you use the expression *Body of Christ,* you do not get "heavenly" minded. This title has to do with the earth. We are, in this context, talking about an earthly relationship with flesh and blood people who go to make up the Body. The scene of action is on the earth. When you say, "I am a member of the Body of Christ", recognize the feet of clay which you have and that these feet are planted in the sin-filled, curse-ridden earth in which we all are living. Here we are face to face with demons, sickness and the tenacity of sin. We are engaged in hand-to-hand combat with these malignant forces.

The other title, the *Bride of Christ,* relates to heaven and the future — the Marriage Supper of the Lamb, and those related and important Kingdom truths.

In this study, we are limiting our consideration to the Body of Christ, that divinely ordained, active and operating expression of the Whole Christ. Once we catch a glimpse of what Jesus had in mind during that Upper Room discussion with His disciples, we can never be the same again. Something happens inside and we find ourselves with a different attitude and relationship to the whole Body of Christ.

This Body is intended to be the most unified entity in all the world. At its core, the Body of Christ is completely unified. It is only out on the periphery where we find the divided, split, segmented portions man has caused the Body to become. The Body was never meant to be like this and it is not necessary for it to continue in this condition. Our privilege in this day is to right the wrongs of the centuries. God has assigned the ministry gifts this function — that of bringing unity to the Body — on the earth!

> *He gave some apostles; and some, prophets; and some evangelists; and some, pastors and teachers; for the perfecting of the saints, for the work of the ministry, for the edifying of the body of Christ: till we all come in the* unity *of the faith, and of the knowledge of the Son of God, unto a perfect man, unto the measure of the stature of the fulness of Christ:* (Ephesians 4:11–13)

Isn't it strange how we can read a certain portion of the Scripture with only one thought in mind. Then, suddenly, new truth is revealed and we wonder how we could have been so blind. One such verse that suddenly took on a truth that revolutionized my thinking is Hebrews 10:7:

> *Then said I, Lo I come (in the volume of the book, it is written of me) to do thy will, O God.*

There was that time when I responded to these words in this way: "Lord, I don't come to do my will. I come to do Your will. I submit, Lord."

But the Lord answered my acknowledgement of submission with these words, "Bob, you are reading that verse all wrong. The emphasis here is not on submission, but on the verb *do.* Read it again."

I did — and what a difference — *"I came to do!"* What is a body for but *to do something?* Wasn't that the purpose for which Jesus came in a physical body — *to do the will of the Father?* Jesus made it very plain that this was why He had come — Luke 4:16—21:

And he came to Nazareth, where he had been brought up, and as his custom was, he went into the synagogue on the sabbath day, and stood up for to read. And there was delivered unto him the book of the prophet Easias. And when he had opened the book, he found the place where it was written, The Spirit of the Lord is upon me, because he hath anointed me to preach the gospel to the poor; he hath sent me to heal the broken-hearted, to preach deliverance to the captives, and recovering of sight to the blind, to set at liberty them that are bruised. And he began to say unto them, This day is the scripture fulfilled in your ears.

The Father, the Son and the Holy Spirit are all interested in the earth because that is where the sick and afflicted are. The anointing of the Holy Spirit which came upon the Lord Jesus was designed to fulfill God's earthly purpose. Jesus was baptized in the Holy Ghost that He might reach out into the world and meet needs. God desires the Church *to do* the work Jesus did. It is our privilege and responsibility to take up the task at the point where Jesus left it to us when He said, ". . . Peace be unto you: as the Father hath sent me, *even so send I you*" (John 20:21).

"I send you" . . . to do . . . to preach the gospel . . . to heal the broken-hearted . . . deliverance . . . recovering of sight to the blind . . . *This day — our day — this scripture is being fulfilled through CHRIST IN SESSION.*

Look with me again at our diagram picturing the Body of Christ — that earthly expression of the Lord Jesus — and beside it is the Bride of Christ — that love relationship which is to be consummated in the future. Is the difference clear in your thinking? The heavenly relationship is very important, but our emphasis here is on the earth. When the Body of Christ is mentioned, please immediately think of a physical relationship of live, warm bodies. The real issue before us is the physical expression of the will of God on the earth. That Body is made up of physical bodies—yours and mine.

Many of the teachings of Paul to the early churches were vitally related to the concept of the Body of Christ. This was something new to their generation. And they found it exciting! Every time Paul talks about the baptism in the Holy Spirit and the gifts of the Spirit, he does so in relation to the Body of Christ and its many-membered function.

Three portions from Paul's letters to the churches demonstrate this. The New Testament Christians were learning what it meant to operate as members of the Body of Christ. Salvation as they understood it was something they possessed and enjoyed together!

I. ". . . *present your bodies a living sacrifice, holy, acceptable unto God:*" *(Romans 12:1 with verse 6)*

The body Paul is talking about here is your physical body — the one you are living in. Present it to the Lord.

You may say, "Well, the Lord doesn't need my body. He just wants my heart." Not, that is not what Paul said. The Lord wants your body so that He may fill it with the power and the presence of His Holy Spirit. Then you will be the container to take Him where He wants to go and do what He wants to do.

Many of us have been learning what it means to be a container. This can get us into some exciting and unusual situations. One day I was called on to counsel with a husband and wife who were believers in the Lord Jesus Christ. When I arrived at the home, there were sounds of a quarrel going on. As I witnessed the antagonism, bitterness and breach that was between those two, something within me cried out, "This is not the will of God!" It was God's Spirit registering anguish at the hurt He was experiencing to see two believers in such a conflict.

My own spirit acknowledged, "No, it isn't!" Because I was serving as God's container, the Holy Spirit came forth in a prophetic ministry. Deliverance and healing followed.

Simply because I had offered my body as an instrument for His use, God was able, through the power of the Holy Spirit, to step into that seemingly impossible situation and bring restoration and peace.

God is looking for bodies to use in solving the problems we find all around us every day.

II. *"For he that eateth and drinketh unworthily, eateth and drinketh judgment to himself, not discerning the Lord's body." (I Corinthians 11:29 with 12:27).*

These words helped me in my "seeing" the Body of Christ. There was a time when I took communion, I would try to *discern* the Lord's body and I would say, "Oh, Lord, I see You hanging on that tree for me."

One day the Lord responded: "Mumford, it's not that One on the tree you are to discern, it's the believer sitting next to you."

Oh! That one sitting next to me was a fellow member of the Lord's Body — and *he* was the one I was to be considering! The discerning of the Lord's Body does not belong in the heavenly realm. It is very earthly and practical, this understanding of the Body of Christ. We will share more of this privilege of "discerning" in our next chapter.

But, do you see that the Body is Methodists, Episcopalians, Pentecostals, tambourines, blacks, whites, yellows, problems, suffering, hunger? Granted, it is much more comfortable to sit in our pews and meditate on Heaven and Jesus, than it is to think about that person next to me. That kind of meditation may lead to my getting involved! I may not even like the one next to me — and that poses a real problem. To avoid spiritual escapism, we are being forced to handle the things on this earth. God, in his wisdom, has provided for this very eventuality!

III. "Now there are diversities of gifts, but the same Spirit. And there are differences of administrations, but the same Lord. And there are diversities of operations, but it is the same God which worketh all in all . . . For the Body is not one member, but many" (I Corinthians 12:4—6 and 14).

Here again is stressed the many-membered Body and the unity in its operation. We are told that by one Spirit we have all been given our particular piece of equipment to enable us to fit into the Body that is to be operational upon the earth.

Everything in our physical body has been placed there for a purpose and each member has its peculiar function to fulfill. Each part is necessary for maximum operation. This principle also applies to the Body of Christ. Each part has been fitted to operate within the whole that we might make up the one Body on earth.

As that one Body comes together, it is to carry on the work that Jesus initiated on the earth. Needs can be met when the Whole Christ comes together. I cannot do it alone and neither can any one else! Some have tried, but it is not God's plan.

This means coming to the place of involvement and acceptance of individual responsibility. It means that all of us — our warm, physical bodies — have to give ourselves to the Holy Spirit and say, "Lord Jesus, fit me into the Body so that it might function."

Only then will CHRIST IN SESSION be enabled to carry out the business for which it was constituted.

Chapter Five

PERCEIVING . . . HIS PEOPLE

One of the privileges of being "His people" is the opportunity to share together as we have been doing. The joining of spirit and mind through the written page draws us into a relationship which we may never be privileged to experience person-to-person. If, however, we have come closer to understanding the meaning of the Body of Christ through these previous chapters, we have accomplished something of eternal value.

DISCERNING THE LORD'S BODY

This brings us to a privilege which Jesus instituted for our mutual enrichment. I refer to what we call *Communion* or the *Lord's Supper*. Here is tied up all of the truths we have been sharing. I am going to ask that we approach this portion of our study together as if we were sitting at the Lord's Table for the purpose of actually sharing in the Supper one with another.

As we sit together around a table — spirits joined in our search for reality — we all realize that some of the deeper implications that Jesus conveyed at that first supper have been lost to us over the years. Paul understood these truths and attempted to impress them upon the hearts of the early believers. I pray that we may re-discover what Jesus, Paul and the first century Christians experienced as they came to meet around a common table to fellowship with one another.

IN JERUSALEM

Our first table is in the Upper Room with Jesus and the Eleven . . . no, there were twelve disciples at the opening of that gathering. Let us listen to Jesus (Luke 22:14—19) as He initiates the Memorial Supper:

> *And when the hour was come, he sat down, and the twelve apostles with him. And he said unto them, With desire I have desired to eat this passover with you before I suffer.* (The word "desire" here is a very strong word . . . it denotes deep longing.) *And he took the cup, and gave thanks, and said, Take this, and divide it among yourselves: And he took bread, and gave thanks, and brake it, and gave unto them saying, This is my body which is given for you; this do in remembrance of me.*

"In remembrance of me". — Only one who *has known,* or experienced, can *remember.* The first requisite for receiving true benefit from the Supper is to *know* Jesus as Lord and Saviour — the One Who shed His blood for the ministry of reconciliation — reconciling man to God.

As He said, "This is my body . . .", and as each one present took a piece of that "body" into his own life, that one became an active participant in the Body that Jesus was to establish on the earth.

Jesus says something in closing that is filled with pathos: "But, behold, the hand of him that betrayeth me is with me on the table." We know that He was referring to Judas and we know of the betrayal that was soon to take place.

Now, to the Oriental mind, the height of insult and injury was to be betrayed by one who was willing to sit at the same table with you and take part in the hospitality you were offering in genuine trust. Can you feel how this must have hurt Jesus that night? Can you feel how it must hurt Him today when we — as members of His Body — sit around the table and take part of His provision for our fellowship with each other and with Him — and then we go out to betray one another?

How do we betray one another? Perhaps not in actual sell-out for thirty pieces of silver to the enemy forces, as did Judas Iscariot; but nevertheless it is the same principle. When we talk disparingly, or critically, or question the motives of our fellow believers — is not this selling out to the enemy? We have mentioned how Satan delights in anything that divides believers — or subtracts from our witness to the world. Remember the admonition of Proverbs 6 concerning "sowing discord among the brethren." Does this thought give us something to seriously consider as we sit here together? It should.

IN CORINTH

Next, let us join Paul as he shares with members of the church of Corinth about proper observance of the Lord's Supper. This communication is by the means of a letter, written in reply to questions raised by the members themselves. They were having problems and turned to their spiritual father for advice. Satan had succeeded in causing divisions and disgraces among these believers and Paul was writing to try to bring them together in Christ.

Our second table, then, is in Corinth with the elders of the local church reading portions of Paul's letter to the members. We will try to see not only the problems they were facing, but how these problems relate to us today. We begin with I Corinthians 11:18.

> *For first of all, when ye come together in the church, I hear that there be divisions among you; and I partly believe it.*

Looking at the factions, schisms and sects within the Church today, we can partly believe, along with Paul, that this is displeasing to God. This is one reason why a changing concept of the Body of Christ — relating it to our own physical bodies — is so vital. The unifying force of love and pure motivation is beginning to bring together a Body which was intended to be *one,* not divided. Unity bears witness to God's power to bring together men despite their fabricated distinctions.

> *For there* must be *also heresies among you, that they which are approved may be made manifest among you.*

The word "heresies" might be expressed as "self-willed opinions". Are not the "divisions" caused only by self — and not by God? Yet in it all, God has a good reason for permitting these "heresies". Through them, the truth shall become recognized. As the Light is turned on, the things of darkness are exposed for what they really are. In comparison with "these things which are approved" — those things which bear God's stamp of approval, — man-made doctrines and opinions will be recognized as only shadow, causing reality to emerge.

> *When you come together therefore into one place, this is not to eat the Lord's supper. For in eating every one taketh before other his own supper; and one is hungry, and another is drunken . . . despise ye the church of God?*

It seems some of the members in Corinth were coming together more on the basis of personal gratification, rather than for the benefit of the Body. Is it possible to prostitute the purpose for which the Supper was instituted? Sure it is. Personal gratification need not take the form of over-eating and too much drinking. It may be that a person allows the Supper to degenerate into merely partaking of "grape juice and crackers", missing entirely what Jesus intended we gain from coming around a common table. What you get out of the observance depends upon what you put into it. When Paul said, ". . . despise ye the church of God?", he was not referring to any man-made building called a "church", but to the Body made possible by the sacrifice of the body of Jesus.

> *And when he had given thanks, he brake it, and said, Take eat: this is my body, which is broken for you: this do in remembrance of me.*

In an earlier portion of this same letter, (10:16–17), Paul wrote, "The bread which we break, is it not the communion of the Body of Christ? For we all are partakers of that one bread." Can you see that Paul was trying to bring about the unity of the believers by showing them they were all "one loaf" — one body? A physical body cannot be segmented and maintain proper operation. We call this physical disruption being handicapped. Just so, the Body of Christ is handicapped when it loses the concept of its inter-dependence. Today, too, we are all "one loaf".

> *So if anyone eats this bread and drinks from this cup of the Lord in an unworthy manner, he is guilty of sin against the body and the blood of the Lord. That is why a man should examine himself carefully before eating the bread and drinking from the cup. For if he eats the bread and drinks from the cup unworthily, not thinking about the body of Christ and what it means, he is eating and drinking God's judgment upon himself; for he is trifling with the death of Christ.* (I Corinthians 11:27—29, Living Letters)

These are strong words. What was Paul trying to express? First, notice that Paul said we were to *examine ourselves*. Aren't we much more apt to examine the person next to us — or that one we disagreed with recently — or that one we may be holding a grudge against? The examination is not how we are related to the Lord — personal sin or failure — an introspection, but *how* are you related to the other members of the same Body?!

Earlier I shared with you the understanding the Lord had given to me about "discerning the Lord's body". He told me the body I was to be thinking about was not primarily His body hanging on the cross, but the body of the person next to me — that fellow member of the "Body". Jesus impressed upon me, "I suffered so you could appreciate and fellowship with the one next to you."

This Body of Christ is so designed that we are dependent upon each other. We *need* to be rightly related — to appreciate and accept each other. We will discover that we cannot get along by ourselves. We must come to recognize the *allos* and the *heteros* — those we like and those who rub us the wrong way. We are all part of His body.

We partake "unworthily" of the Supper when we cannot say in our hearts, "Brother, I believe you are a member of the Body. I receive ministry from you." Paul is saying, "Don't partake of the Supper until you examine your relationship to the other members of the Body." He makes it plain that we are "condemning" ourselves when we know we are not rightly related to others who are sharing in the fellowship. We are "betraying" our Lord and our brother when we harbor malice . . . distrust . . . disdain.

> *That is why many of you are weak and
> sick, and some have even died.*

For what cause? Because of *not understanding* the Body. Some fail to acknowledge the value and placement of other members in the same fellowship. We may even refuse ministry from someone with whom we do not agree or who has offended us in some way. For this reason we may have missed out on healing that would have been available to us through that one we disregarded. Remember the pastor who rejected the ministry of healing because of the *one* it was who came forward to pray for him?

There is also the possibility that some were sickly in the fellowship at Corinth because the stronger ones were neglecting their ministry to the weaker ones. "And many have died an untimely death — or prematurely." This neglect has resulted in death for some.

Either rejection of other's ministry or lack of assuming responsibility to minister causes physical damage, as well as spiritual loss.

> *For if we would judge ourselves, we should not be judged. But when we are judged, we are chastened of the Lord, that we should not be condemned with the world.*

If we examine ourselves and find some areas where we are lacking in the love and appreciation we should have for others, we can get busy and do something about it — acknowledge it and right the wrongs. Through this chastening of the Lord, this examining of ourselves, we may be sparing ourselves untold misery and strife. God provides every opportunity to recognize and deal with sins which crop up in our lives. This is one very real and practical way.

> *Wherefore, my brethren, when ye come together to eat, tarry one for another.*

There is compassion in that phrase, "tarry one for another". If we would stop and consider the burden a brother or sister might be carrying, what a difference it could make in the Body. You don't love people because you want to. We love because we have to. God knows our need to *learn* to love. He instituted this Supper so that when we came together we would be confronted by our lack of love and concern for others. That's the way the Body works. When concern and love become uppermost in our relationships, there is a tie that binds. There are, as well, spiritual gifts made available to enable us to minister to each other, as well as to a needy world.

But the manifestation of the Spirit is given to every man to profit withal . . . But all of these worketh that one and the selfsame Spirit, dividing to every man severally as he will.

These are leveling thoughts. There is no room for pride in the manifestation of the gifts. The Spirit gave them as He saw fit. They are for the profit of all the members. As we come to accept the sovereign operation of the Spirit, plus the need for each other, we experience what Jesus intended for us to experience — *inter-dependence.* God set every member in place. He has a specific design in mind — "as it pleased him". The more we acknowledge this, the more we discover the Body of Christ is bigger and different than we initially understood it to be.

Nay, much more those members of the body, which seem to be more feeble are necessary: and those members of the body, which we think to be less honorable, upon these we bestow more abundant honor; and our uncomely parts have more abundant comliness. For our comely parts have no need. But God hath tempered the body together, having given more abundant honor to that part which lacked: That there should be

*no schism in that body; but that the members
should have the same care one for another.*

Clearly, a warning about looking down on some
members we might consider insignificant (feeble).
Watch yourself! We cannot say, "I do not have any
need of that person!" Or, "I don't like this
person." That person is a part of the same Body
that you are. God said some of the more feeble are
necessary. Who are we to look down upon him if
God considers him important to the working of His
Body? We might *say* "we have no need of him",
only to discover that we couldn't get away with
such an attitude. God, in His infinite wisdom, has
shut us up together!

Let me ask, did you notice the words, "tempered the body together"? Tempered carries the
picture of the heat being applied, doesn't it? God
knows just how to "temper" and He will not spare
bringing pressure to bear. *Why did He temper us
together?* That there be no schism — no break in
the fellowship. We must learn to have concern and
care for each other. Involvement is necessary. God
has seen to it.

*And whether one member suffer, all the
members suffer with it; or one member be
honored, all the members rejoice with it.*

What a revelation of relationship! Ask yourself
— does the suffering of a brother affect me in any
way? It is easy to listen to requests for prayer
being read — and then forget all about it. The
privilege to pray for one another may represent the
least we can do in a situation. Of course, there is
the possibility we could get involved in meeting the
need if we pray. Have you *ever* suffered when

someone else was ill . . . injured . . . known financial loss? Most of us think we have enough suffering of our own to do. But this is not the way the Body is to respond.

The same goes for honor. Do you rejoice in another's good fortune . . . promotion . . . public acclaim? Or does jealousy take the place of joy in another's time of blessing?

Paul has been unfolding how CHRIST IN SESSION works. Has your understanding and appreciation of the Body been enlarged through his letter? Did you catch the heartbeat, not only of Paul but also of Jesus Himself, at this second table? If you did, I would like to suggest that we go one more step together.

IN REMEMBRANCE OF HIM

Gather with me around a *third* table. We are meeting in this book as fellow members of the Body of Christ. Picture on our table one large loaf of bread. May I ask that each of us break a portion from that loaf and as we hold it in our hands that we consider together some further aspects of the Whole Christ. We can now fellowship in Spirit and Truth. This is one of the privileges of being members of the Body — CHRIST IN SESSION.

I am going to offer you a piece of my portion of bread and ask that you, in return accept it — and offer me a portion of yours. As we do this, let us make some commitments to each other and to Christ.

Friend, I believe you are a member of the

same Body of which I am a member. I receive you . . . I admit that I need you . . . I receive ministry from you.

As I eat this piece of bread which you have given me, I acknowledge that we are breaking bread together in remembrance of our Lord Jesus Christ. He gave His life that we might enjoy this privilege. I realize that I now have within me the same bread that you have in you. We are one with another — we are one with Him. He *died* to purchase this privilege for us.

He made possible a love for each other, too. I might not love you in the natural. You might not love me. God knew that and provided the means whereby, as we share together of His Body, we can develop and experience a reciprocal love. He will give strength and grace so that we might rejoice together. He made it possible that we will not betray one another — that we will not be jealous. He has provided forgiveness and cleansing for us.

For we are many members — but one Body. Do you hear Christ pleading, "Church if you want this thing to function, just get together!"

Here is reality. Right here around the Lord's Table — discerning the Lord's Body — each — other — here all of our needs are met. Here is reality in relationship.

As we partake of this one loaf in faith, Jesus will do two things for us. He will forgive us of all sin, especially sin against the Body.

And He will give us grace to embrace this concept of CHRIST IN SESSION, as well as find
and function in our own spiritual responsibility.

Chapter Six

PURSUING . . . THE GOAL

Let us ask ourselves some questions before we move into some of the other privileges and blessings that are ours because we are "one body".

1. Do you feel that you have made headway in determining just what is *shadow* and what is *substance* in your own particular situation? Unless we feel individually enlightened, this will turn out to be just "another book".

2. Do you feel that you have a better understanding of what Jesus was talking about as He met with His disciples that last night in the Upper Room? Have you caught the vision and fulfillment of *"I will go away . . . I will come again"*?

3. Do you feel better acquainted with the *Program* that was initiated as Jesus went away and the Holy Spirit brought Him back to the believers who were gathered together and waiting for the promise of the Father? Do you see this *Program* in operation today?

4. Do you feel more desire to be a part of what God is doing today? Has *Progress* been made in your grasp of the meaning of relationship to other members of the Body?

5. Do you understand in a more practical sense what it means to *perceive* the Lord's Body? Have the advantages and disadvantages of discerning the Lord's Body been made clear to you?

We could ask many more questions. These are just a means to start us thinking and responding. For response is one sign of spiritual growth. In fact, it is only as individuals respond that CHRIST IN SESSION can be maintained, and thus carry out the business at hand. That business? "Sirs, We would see Jesus." We are to present Jesus to the world — *His character, His power, and His authority.* This business demands the participation of every member.

EVERY MEMBER INVOLVEMENT

These words may sound like a slogan for a campaign. In a way it is. It is important that every member come to see the privilege of involvement — understand the value and necessity! Paul had this in mind when he wrote these words to the believers in Rome: (Romans 12:3—5)

For I say, through the grace given unto me to every man that is among you, not to think of himself more highly than he ought to think; but to think soberly, according as God

hath dealt to every man the measure of faith.
For as we have many members in one body,
and all members have not the same office: so
we, being many are one body in Christ, and
every one members one of another.

Yes, every man and woman has been given a
certain "measure" or "portion" of faith. God has
given you, as a member of the Body, a responsibility. Each one of us is required to take this
responsibility by faith and begin to move out and
minister in the particular realm and area to which
God has called us. Not one of us can any longer
continue to sit in the grandstand. You can't hire
me to do your work any more than I can expect
you to do mine. God has called a whole Body — a
many-membered Body. This earthly relationship
must be recognized and embraced. God is bringing
the Body together. Needs can only be met when
the Whole Christ is presented to the world — and
that forces each one of us to accept his placement
and responsibility.

INVOLVEMENT – TO WHAT EXTENT?

All right, we acknowledge the need, but to what
degree are we going to extend ourselves? What
holds us back from getting involved when we know
we should? Could it be because we know when we
place our bodies at the disposal of Christ, we in-
volve personal convenience, our pocketbooks, our
family activities, our business — all that we have
and are?

The giving of the material — tithes and offerings
— is easier than to offer our bodies, isn't it? Most

of us would rather increase our tithe than give the obedience He is seeking. Which is shadow and which is substance in this issue? Hebrews 10:5 sheds some light on the answer:

> *Sacrifice and offerings thou wouldest not, but a body that hast prepared me.*

God knows that when we bring our bodies to Him, our finances are His as a fringe benefit! So is our time, energy and influence.

INGREDIENTS OF INVOLVEMENT

First, it requires proper motivation. Almost from our spiritual birth we are taught to come to Christ for what He will do *for* us. Involvement is the very opposite! We must enter the Body concepts with a whole-hearted desire to give, do and be — not concerned for what we can get out of it. As we "lose our life" for the good of the whole, out of it comes the reality and the supply for which we have so desperately sought.

Second, involvement demands a certain mental preparation. Once involvement is desired and sought, the Lord Jesus Christ proceeds to break down barriers, prejudices and foolishness that hinders me from placement in the Body. This is done in the laboratory of human experience and is often frightening and painful.

Thirdly, it requires a cessation of the spiritual "long ranger" concept. Most of us, frustrated at the division, confusion and bickering in the Body of Christ, solved the problem by withdrawing from people, fellowship and conflict. Shut up to ourselves and to God, it may seem that our problems had lessened. Involvement means you have discovered — irrevocably — that you cannot be truly spiritual *alone*. However frustrating and complicated it seems, we now labor for the whole Christ — bringing my portion into proper relationship with others who are next to me.

Fourthly, there is a prerequisite for involvement: the necessity for an attitude of *expectancy* and *teachableness*. For years men have gathered around certain experiences (i.e., salvation, the Holy Spirit, etc.), or even certain doctrines (i.e., Calvinism, pre-millenialism, etc.). Prophetically, the scriptures declare the day when "unto him shall the gathering of the people be" (Genesis 49:10). Involvement requires you to understand that God has many new and exciting things ahead for Christ's Body. Can you believe that there are things on God's agenda which we do not yet know? By these words "new and exciting" I do not mean some sensational, extra-biblical experience. Nor do we mean some emotional, temporary upheaval. We do mean *significant* and *radical change* in the Church of Jesus Christ, which is His Body.

Once we felt safe and secure in whatever denomination we happened to be. We felt ours was "the thing that God was doing". Suddenly we are finding out that God has no favorites. Color . . . creed . . . race . . . social status . . .education — these barriers are tumbling due to the present movement of the Spirit. For years we sang about unity but seldom was it seen in practice. Unity does not mean uniformity. Yet, this "coming together" disturbs our theology. Let us remember it this way:

Conformity is not unity;
Diversity is not disunity.

Many of us believe the fulfillment of the promise, "I will pour out my spirit upon all flesh . . ." (Acts 2:17) has only just begun. Did you know that in Indonesia thousands of Moslems have come to know Jesus Christ as Saviour? There have only been a handful of Moslems accept Christ in the two thousand years of church history! We see Christ invading places where we didn't think He would ever go! We are seeing the Lord Jesus baptize people in the Holy Spirit – people we were taught in seminary to avoid! This is a shock to religious and doctrinal preconceptions. Don't be put off by some who feel this movement to be the forerunner of a "world church" in some organizational sense. A "world church" may arise on the scene of world history, but it will be as a reaction to the unity seen by all in the spiritual Body of Christ (John 17:23).

This is an amazing day in which we live. It is a challenge to see so many of God's children coming together – motivated simply by the love we share for the Lord Jesus. We are not drawn together to "build" anything of a physical nature – no more shadows behind which we can take refuge. No, we want the *substance;* we want to see the building up of the spiritual Body of Christ (Ephesians 2:22).

IGNORANCE – HOW TO DEAL WITH IT

God thinks of everything, doesn't He? He recognized the possibility of acting out of ignorance and provided for restitution when one realized his ignorance. In Leviticus chapter 4, Moses told the Israelites, at the command of God, just how to handle the situation. A certain kind of "offering" was instituted for their "ignorance". God accepted the offering and man was expected to move forward in his new knowledge . . . "If ye do this from ignorance, you can offer a sacrifice . . ."

This brings me to confess before you that for years I considered myself "God's defender of the Faith"! And there are many others who fall into this self-appointed category. When I found someone who didn't understand things as I saw them, or if they didn't line up according to my self-sustained rules and regulations, I was apt to be critical and judgmental.

Then one day while reading some of Paul's letters to the early churches, I caught the implication of this words, "I would not have you to be ignorant, brethren . . ." These words are found, not once, but thirteen or fourteen times. He reiterates over and over again that he doesn't want his people to be ignorant about spiritual things. Paul was not critical or judgmental, he truly did not want them to be ignorant! What he understood that I did not, was that most people act the way they do because they are spiritually ignorant.

How many of us realize how "ignorant" *we* are when it comes to spiritual truths? When we study, we find out how much we do not understand. The more we study, the more there seems to be to understand. This is the challenge of the Word of God. When I came asking, "Lord, teach me about spiritual things," He began to show me how *ignorant* I was. He also showed me how many times we act like Peter — willing to grab the sword and cut off an ear in what we feel is God's defense. But He tells us, as He told Peter, to put up our swords. Unity is to be our motive.

If we will be honest, we will all admit to doing things and saying things simply because we did not know any better — ignorance. One of the prayers throughout the Body of Christ is, "Lord, teach us Your ways. We offer to You the sacrifice of ignorance. We have not understood Your ways."

Paul tells us that ". . . we know in part and prophesy in part . . . we see through a glass darkly." Both of these remarks were made in I Corinthians chapter 13 where he was teaching on love. Someday we will see it all as it really is. Until then, we must be freed from religious and doctrinal dogmatism. We often act in ignorance and immaturity as if we were the final authority, and that our church knew and had it all.

Quite a few years ago, in a dream, I was shown a huge Bible. It seemed to come down out of Heaven and I remember trying to reach up to see into that Bible. I was curious to know where it was opened — and what was on those pages before me. It seemed inside that Bible were large pages and some smaller ones. In desperation, I cried, "Lord, what are those smaller pages?"

The impression which came to me was, "The smaller pages are the Books to the Corinthians that have not as yet been fully opened to the Church." Then I became determined to study in a systematic manner the epistles of Paul to the Corinthian church. Much of what we refer to as the Charismatic renewal has been opened to us through these books. In these epistles, Paul teaches about the things which we are experiencing today.

Since then, I have discovered that God was giving this same direction to other men. Together, as we study, God has been opening truths — nothing new — but new to us. I read in Chapter 3 of I Corinthians, "for all things are yours." Did you know that the baptism in the Holy Spirit is not a new experience? It is one of "those things that are yours". We were not aware of the the ministry of the Holy Spirit in this manner previously. This process is called "restoration". It is God restoring truth that has been "lost". This is what Luther, Calvin and Wesley experienced in their day. Bible scholars are continually "discovering" latent truth in the pages of the New Testament. Many of these teachings are directly related to church life . . . the Body of Christ.

WHICH ARE YOU SEEING — ADAM OR CHRIST?

On the next page is a diagram which will help us in "seeing" two truths which are closely related: (1) from singular to plural; (2) from Adam to Christ.

Notice that Jesus, on the left side of the diagram, is the Jesus of the Gospels. We have one Jesus Christ. He is in a physical body. He could go to Galilee and Samaria and Jerusalem at will. But He was limited to one place at one time. He took away His first form (No. 1) that He might give us His second (No. 2). Here, pictured on the right-

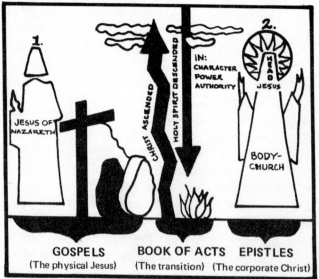

GOSPELS   **BOOK OF ACTS**   **EPISTLES**
(The physical Jesus)   (The transition)   (The corporate Christ)

hand side of the diagram, we have a completely different understanding of Christ. As presented in the Epistles, we have Jesus Christ — Head and Body. This Body is a many-membered operation. It is you and it is I.   The Body is God's creation, just as our human bodies are God's creation. There is diversity and unity within its nature. The Holy Spirit is the very Breath which gives life to this Body.

Jesus took No. 1 *from the earth* that He might establish No. 2 *on the earth.* The singular became plural!

The connecting link between the singular Christ and the plural Christ was the Holy Spirit. When Jesus ascended He took with Him the *power and authority and character of Himself.* When the Holy Spirit descended ten days later. He brought back the things of Jesus and He distributed them. He continues to distribute these same things — *the power, authority and character* to believers today. The Corporate Christ is CHRIST IN SESSION. Consider these verses from II Corinthians 5:16—18:

> *Wherefore henceforth know we no man after the flesh; yea, though we have known Christ after the flesh, yet now henceforth know we him no more. Therefore if any man be in Christ he is a new creature: old things are passed away; behold, all things are become new. And all things are of God, who reconciled us to himself by Jesus Christ, and hath given us the ministry of reconciliation.*

Even though we cannot know Jesus "after the flesh", we can know Him in His larger ministry — through His Body, the Church. Here is the practical outworking of God's will in the earth day by day. *Here is His legislative Body — character, power and authority.*

Once I worshipped Jesus of Nazareth. He was to me a Man — a Person. Please do not misunderstand me. I still love Jesus, my Saviour. But, as Paul tells us, "Once we knew Christ after the flesh . . ." Paul asks us to take into consideration that we cannot *fully* know Him in that dimension *only* any more. We are told, ". . . if any man be in Christ, he is a new creature." I want us to see that following the transition period of Acts (as shown on the diagram), I can love Jesus not just as the Man, but as the Head of the Body — as well as all the "new creatures" who make up His Body. Remember, though, that here we are emphasizing the spiritual aspect of Christ, but not to the rejection of the natural man Christ Jesus. This follows the

Apostle Paul's admonition in I Corinthians 15:46:
"That is not first which is spiritual, but that which
is natural; then that which is spiritual follows."
(ASV)

Here we come to our second truth. Paul is teaching us in the scripture we have shared, that there is
an attitude we must assume toward the members
of the Body.

Someone may say, "I'm a new creature. The
Bible says it, and I believe it." We may not see
much "new" in that person – or anything to get
particularly excited about. In fact, we may have to
exercise our faith to believe any "newness" at all.
Remember that his "newness" may require some
breathing room and some "special handling" as he
moves over into new realms, meets up with new
rules and adjusts to new relationships. Don't judge
too harshly! Paul is telling us, "When you meet a
man or woman, what are you going to look for –
the old creation or the new? If you are going to
look for the old man (the Adam in a man) . . . the
old flesh . . . you are going to see just that."

What a glorious day it will be when we stop
looking for the Adam in every man or woman. If
we can see there is *one* Body, *one* faith, *one* Lord
– and begin to see people, not after the flesh, but
after the new creature . . . when we begin to
search out the Christ in them . . . what a difference this will make in our whole outlook on our
fellow believers.

Here we are – a group small or large getting
together for fellowship. Each one present has problems. If you are looking for the Adam, you will
find complications and failures. But if you decide

to recognize that when Jesus came back to the earth as Head, He made each one present a part of the Body — that becomes a matter for serious consideration. Since I am a part of the Body of Christ, you had better watch how you treat me. Jesus received me just like I am — faults, problems and hang-ups. He is helping me get rid of some of them — for which I am grateful. But as you look at me, you can look for the Adam — or you can look for Jesus — signs of His new nature!

The same thing goes as I look at those with whom I associate and to whom I minister. It is true for each member of the Body as he relates to others in his fellowship or church. This *acceptance in Christ* affects the way in which one individual can minister to another. In places where people receive me as a man of God, the ministry can flow. Or they may say, "Mumford! Man, I used to know him when he rode a motorcycle! Can any good things come out of New Jersey?" I rode a motorcycle once a long time ago — that was B.C. Spiritually, we must gain a different perspective.

If you will ask God to alter your perspective and look at every believer as "a new creature in Christ" — a fellow member of the Body, your spirit will leap within you when the two of you meet and you will find yourself saying truthfully, "Brother, it is good to see you." It is this spirit-meeting-spirit that binds us together as one Body. It is the organic unity of the vine and the branches in demonstration. The Holy Spirit makes it possible for us to join forces and operate as CHRIST IN SESSION. Do you see here a practical outworking of a deep spiritual truth?

As we grow in this understanding we will look upon others — be they "same kind" or "different kind" — as a part of ourselves. This kind of vision will cause us to realize that one's wife or husband — child or neighbor — is a part of the same Body that you are. What hurts him will be to your hurt. His every advance is your advance.

When you look upon a person with the eyes of Christ and treat that person as a part of Christ, that person acts and reacts differently. Did you know that? This is reciprocal love, the atmosphere which brings out the new nature of Christ within the other person. There is a response that upbuilds and rejoices *mutually.*

*   *   *

As your life touches the believer next to you — be it in a church meeting, at the grocery store or the office — consider that you are beholding a part of the Body of Christ. Amazing things can and will happen as we change our attitude. Once this basic understanding becomes reality in your life, you are prepared to move ahead in unfolding this truth to others and demonstrating CHRIST IN SESSION!

HELPS ALONG THE WAY

The Body of Christ is the Church Universal. It is made up of all believers in Jesus Christ.

The churches are the ecclesia . . . assemblies . . . gatherings of individuals. These may be duly called to meet at set times, or as occasion demands.

Unity of churches is different than spiritual unity of the Body.

The Church (Body of Christ) and the churches are *not* interchanging terms.

The Body functions continually. It functions not by compulsion, membership or commitment to a single creed. Rather it is individuals who, by recognizing the corporeate necessity, voluntarily submit themselves, their ministry and leadings to the good of the whole. This desire for the well-being of the other members becomes a heart cry and true Body concept is born in the midst of the people.

The Body is not a coming together of perfect people, but ones who have sought out placement and function in order to progress and mature in spiritual growth.

Whatever your church (or larger fellowship), do not omit the cell group as a basis and beginning of fellowship.

HELPS ALONG THE WAY *(Con'd)*

The power of the Body of Christ lies in the corporeate expression of its many-membered fellowship.

The gifts of the Spirit are the tools given to us to do God's work in God's way. The presence of the various gifts are, by scriptural injunction, found in every Bible-believing, Spirit-filled fellowship.

The problem is (1) recognizing this potential, (2) developing it to a full expression of the Whole Christ.

The result is productivity through the proper use of the talent, life, anointing of the Holy Spirit on the individual toward his growth, growth and well-being of others, as well as world evangelism.

THE WHOLE CHRIST:

CHARACTER	POWER	AUTHORITY
Gal. 5:22–23	*I Cor. 12:8–10*	*Eph. 4:11–12*
Love	Word of Wisdom	Apostle
Joy	Word of Knowledge	Prophet
Peace	Faith	Evangelist
Longsuffering	Healing	Pastor
Gentleness	Miracles	Teacher
Goodness	Prophecy	
Faith	Discerning of Spirits	
Meekness	Tongues	
Temperance	Interpretation of Tongues	

RECOMMENDATION

May I recommend a most significant recording which illustrates Christ in Session. It is entitled, "Come Together" by Jimmy Owens with Pat Boone, released through Word Records.